AF228630

INNOVATIONS IN HOCKEY

by Douglas Hustad

SportsZone

An Imprint of Abdo Publishing
abdobooks.com

abdobooks.com

Published by Abdo Publishing, a division of ABDO, PO Box 398166, Minneapolis, Minnesota 55439. Copyright © 2022 by Abdo Consulting Group, Inc. International copyrights reserved in all countries. No part of this book may be reproduced in any form without written permission from the publisher. SportsZone™ is a trademark and logo of Abdo Publishing.

Printed in the United States of America, North Mankato, Minnesota.
102021
012022

Cover Photo: Winslow Townson/AP Images, left; AP Images, right
Interior Photos: Dea/Biblioteca Ambrosiana/De Agostini/Getty Images, 5; Corbis Historical/Getty Images, 7; Shutterstock Images, 10–11; Vince Talotta/Toronto Star/Getty Images, 13; Edward Kitch/AP Images, 15; Julio Cortez/AP Images, 16; Aaron Doster/Cal Sport Media/AP Images, 18; David Zalubowski/AP Images, 21; Darryl Dyck/The Canadian Press/AP Images, 23, 42; Peter Joneleit/Cal Sport Media/AP Images, 26; Michael Ainsworth/AP Images, 29; Yale Joel/The LIFE Picture Collection/Getty Images, 30; Mark Humphrey/AP Images, 32–33; Richard Ulreich/Cal Sport Media/Zuma Wire/AP Images, 34; George Silk/The LIFE Picture Collection/Getty Images, 37; Mike Groll/Zuma Wire/Cal Sport Media/AP Images, 39; Paul Beaty/AP Images, 41

Editor: Katie Chanez
Series Designer: Joshua Olson

Library of Congress Control Number: 2020949107

Publisher's Cataloging-in-Publication Data

Names: Hustad, Douglas, author.
Title: Innovations in hockey / by Douglas Hustad
Description: Minneapolis, Minnesota : Abdo Publishing, 2022 | Series: Sports innovations | Includes online resources and index.
Identifiers: ISBN 9781532195051 (lib. bdg.) | ISBN 9781098215361 (ebook)
Subjects: LCSH: Hockey--Juvenile literature. | Technological innovations--Juvenile literature. | Sports sciences--Juvenile literature. | Performance technology--Juvenile literature. | Hockey--Equipment and supplies--Juvenile literature. | Sports--Juvenile literature.
Classification: DDC 688.76--dc23

TABLE OF CONTENTS

THE
COOLEST GAME

When hockey became popular in the 1800s, players didn't have to spend their time worrying finding a place to play an informal game. After a few good nights of freezing winter temperatures, they had a rink to play on. Any frozen lake, pond, or river could be the site of their next game or practice.

But hockey gradually evolved. The sport became more professional. It grew from a casual game that people played for fun into something more organized.

James Creighton is credited with organizing the first indoor hockey game on March 3, 1875, in Montreal, Quebec. It was held at the Victoria Skating Rink. The game was forced to end early after recreational skaters complained that the hockey players were encroaching on their ice time. But the fans enjoyed it.

caption:

The Victoria Skating Rink in Montreal was a popular winter destination even before it hosted the first indoor hockey game.

Indoor rinks were essential to the development of hockey. Lord Stanley of Preston, a Canadian politician, saw his first hockey game at the Victoria rink in 1889. He went on to donate the trophy that became the Stanley Cup. The first Stanley Cup playoffs were held at the rink in 1894.

The Victoria rink set the standard dimensions of a hockey rink. The surface area of a frozen lake or pond was virtually unlimited. But an indoor rink was different. In the case of the Victoria rink, the ice stretched from Stanley Street to Drummond Street, approximately 200 feet (61 m). All indoor rinks roughly followed that size in the years to come.

STAYING FROZEN

Even though hockey had moved indoors, that didn't solve one major problem. The Victoria rink still depended on the weather to make ice. In the summer, the ice would melt.

An early attempt at a permanent ice rink was unveiled in 1844. The Glaciarium in the United Kingdom used a frozen mix of pig fat and salt. However, the artificial ice smelled terrible, and the rink closed within a year.

Inventor John Gamgee came up with a better idea. He opened a second Glaciarium in 1876. He ran copper pipes under the surface that carried chemicals that stayed cold.

The first Glaciarium was one of the first permanent ice rinks in the world.

These chemicals constantly circulated under the ice and kept it frozen.

That technology is similar to what is used in hockey rinks today. The chemicals have changed, but modern ice stays frozen with the help of thousands of gallons of freezing-cold liquid pumping beneath it. This technology is so effective that it allows hockey to be played almost anywhere, including very warm places.

Since 2008, the National Hockey League (NHL) has scheduled an annual outdoor game called the Winter Classic. It is held in January. Usually, the game is held in a city with a cold climate, so making ice is no problem. But the game has also been held in warmer cities such as Dallas and Saint Louis. The cooling system is able to keep the ice at a steady 22 degrees Fahrenheit (-6°C).

SMOOTH SAILING

Indoor, refrigerated ice changed hockey forever. But it still wasn't perfect. Ice gets choppy and uneven the more it is used.

The players' skates dig into the ice, causing pits and ruts. This was a problem for hockey, as it requires a smooth surface for the puck to move consistently.

Ice-refrigeration pioneer Frank Zamboni owned a rink called Iceland in Southern California. It opened in 1940. In those days, it took a crew of four or five people to smooth out the ice. A tractor would drive over the ice pulling a trailer with a scraper. It shaved off ice that had become rough. Workers trailing the tractor would then spray down the scraped surface with water. To make it smooth, they had to wipe and respray the ice several times. The process took more than an hour.

Zamboni wanted to figure out a way to smooth out the ice faster. For five years he tried different methods. Then, in 1947, he found one that worked. He designed a machine that could do all the tasks at once. Zamboni's machine shaved the ice down, dumped the shavings in a holding tank, laid down a layer of water, and smoothed out the new surface as it drove. Zamboni's machine completed the job in just 15 minutes

Zamboni perfected his design in 1949. The Zamboni Company began manufacturing the machines a year later. In 1954 the machine was first used during an NHL game. Today, Zamboni has sold more than 10,000 ice resurfacers. They are seen during intermissions of nearly every hockey game

Ice resurfacers are now a common sight at hockey games and skating rinks.

around the world. They are often brightly colored, or decorated with the names of teams or the stadium. The NHL requires the ice to be resurfaced between every period, as well as before

and after every game. Two modern machines can resurface the
entire rink in approximately three minutes. The ice resurfacers
are as much a part of the modern game of hockey as sticks,
pucks, and goals.

CHAPTER 2

STICK WITH IT

Nobody knows exactly when the first hockey stick was created. But the oldest existing stick dates back a long way. And surprisingly it's not too different from the sticks that are used today.

That old hockey stick sits in the Canadian Museum of History in Gatineau, Quebec. It belonged to a Nova Scotia man named William "Dilly" Moffatt. Moffatt was born in 1829. His stick was carved from a single sugar maple tree, likely by the Mi'kmaq people of Nova Scotia. Their hand-carved sticks were popular for decades. The Moffatt stick is where the story of the modern hockey stick begins.

Since then, many people have had a hand in innovating the way sticks are made and used. The stick has evolved along with the game.

caption: One of the oldest hockey sticks in the world is on display at Wayne Gretzky's restaurant in Toronto.

Gretzk

BENDING THE BLADE

In the early days, the long, straight blade on the sticks made it harder to maintain control of the puck and make precision passes and shots. Eventually players began experimenting with bending the blades on their sticks to get more control on shots. Early results were mixed. Then a stroke of luck paved the way for one of the game's most important innovations.

Chicago Blackhawks legends Bobby Hull and Stan Mikita were working on their shots after practice one day in the early 1960s. At some point, Mikita's stick blade cracked. It left the blade in a curved shape. Mikita kept using the broken stick and found that he liked the results it produced.

Hull and Mikita began looking for new ways to bend the stick blades. They soaked the blades in hot water and pinned them into door jambs. When Hull and Mikita began using the curved blades in games, they found they had an easier time controlling the puck. Even better, it was easier to lift the puck off the ice when they shot it. Goalies had a hard time stopping their shots, and both players became offensive stars. Hull won the NHL goal-scoring title seven times in the 1960s. Mikita led the league in points (goals plus assists) four times between 1964 and 1968.

Blackhawks forward Stan Mikita helped popularize curved blades.

NHL players now use custom-made sticks.

It didn't take long for the rest of the NHL to catch on and follow the trend. The blades of this era were curved so much they were often referred to as "banana blades." In 1967 the NHL made a rule limiting how much a blade could be curved. But the curved blade was here to stay.

MOVING BEYOND WOOD

One constant for years was the material used to make sticks. Ever since the Mi'kmaq people carved them out of sugar maple, wood was the go-to choice. Until the 1960s, the only major change was the use of harder woods such as ash and birch.

Stick manufacturers Sher-Wood and Canadien added fiberglass to the blades in the 1960s. That made them stronger and less likely to break. Fiberglass also enabled the manufacturers to use lightweight woods such as aspen rather than ash or birch. The Sher-Wood P.M.P. 5030 of the 1970s was one of the most popular sticks ever. It helped the company dominate the market.

Defenseman Adrian Aucoin, who finished his career in 2013 with the Columbus Blue Jackets, was one of the last NHL players to use a wooden stick.

The Easton company made a name for itself by manufacturing aluminum baseball bats in the 1970s. It brought that technology to hockey sticks in the 1980s. The blades remained wood, but the aluminum shafts were lighter and stronger than anything that had come before. These types of sticks became more popular when the legendary Wayne Gretzky played with one.

Easton further refined its technology in the mid-1990s with the use of composite materials. The company engineered a blend of wood, graphite, fiberglass, and other materials to produce an even lighter blade. In 2001 the company released the first fully composite stick. Instead of a separate blade and shaft, the single piece helped players get a great feel for the puck. The sticks had a lot of flex in the shaft so players could put even more power behind their shots. Wooden sticks were once a fixture in the game, but they vanished from the NHL entirely by 2010.

CHAPTER 3

MAKING THE
MODERN NHL

Many things make hockey unique from other sports. Games are played on ice. Standings are based on points instead of a win-loss record. And it has a unique way of deciding tie games.

For many years, the NHL didn't have tiebreakers. The early days of the league featured an overtime period, but it was eliminated in 1942. The league did so to shorten games during World War II (1939–1945), when train schedules were restricted due to the war effort.

From then on, regular-season games that were tied after 60 minutes of play went into the books as ties. Overtime didn't return for 40 years. Finally, a five-minute, five-on-five sudden death overtime was added for the 1983–84 season.

Gary Bettman became commissioner of the NHL in 1993. Bettman tried to make the league more exciting for fans

caption: Tied regular-season games now go into overtime, giving teams another chance to win.

and make the game more popular. One of his strategies was to increase scoring. In 1999 the NHL reduced the number of skaters to four per team during the overtime period. Fewer skaters meant more open ice, leading to more goal-scoring opportunities.

ONE-ON-ONE HOCKEY

Even four-on-four hockey didn't significantly reduce the number of ties, however. So the league further refined its approach. In 2005–06, the league got rid of ties. Overtime stayed the same, but if nobody scored in five minutes of play, the game would be decided by a shootout.

Shootouts had been a feature of international hockey since 1992. They were used that year at the Winter Olympics. Shootouts are an exciting way to end a hockey game. Each team picks three shooters to face the opposing goalie one-on-one. Fans usually stand and cheer as they watch their hometown team try to pull off the win.

But shootouts are also a bit random. Even the best scorers don't succeed much more than 50 percent of the time. And it narrows down an entire game into an individual contest between two players.

a game. But if the game went to overtime, the losing team earned one point.

The new system meant teams could more easily earn points. That kept them in the playoff race longer. But as time went on, many teams did not like the point system combined with a shootout. Because the results of shootouts are somewhat random, they questioned the legitimacy of the extra point awarded to the winner.

Starting in 2015–16, Bettman and the NHL changed the overtime rules again. Each team would only have three skaters on the ice at a time. That created even more open space and scoring opportunities. Fewer games went to a shootout. In the first year of three-on-three, 61.1 percent of overtime games were decided without a shootout, compared to 44.4 percent in the last season of four-on-four overtime. And three-on-three hockey was thrilling to watch for fans.

THE SKATERS IN STRIPES

NHL officials looked and sounded quite different in the league's early days. Before the NHL, officials wore suits and ties. They rang bells instead of blowing whistles when there was a penalty. Later they donned sweaters but kept the ties. It wasn't until the 1950s that they started wearing the vertical stripes they still wear today.

Hockey officials consist of referees and linesmen. Linesmen mostly operate between the two blue lines of a hockey rink. Their main duty is to call icing and offsides violations. Referees are tasked with calling penalties.

For years, most hockey leagues operated with one referee and two linesmen. The NHL was the first league to add a second referee in 1998–99. Most other major leagues around the world have done the same since.

INSTANT REPLAY

Sometimes the on-ice officials need a helping hand. Until the 2019–20 season, a goal judge sat in a booth behind each net. The goal judge switched on a big red light when a puck crossed the goal line.

Starting in the 2019–20 season, the NHL expanded the types of calls that could be reviewed by instant replay.

Goal judges became unnecessary with the expansion of instant replay. The NHL was one of the first North American sports leagues to use instant replay. NHL instant replay debuted in 1991. At first, it was used only when it was unclear if a puck crossed the goal line. Its role has gradually expanded since then. Today, the on-ice referees don't have the final say on disputed calls. The league has a video review system at its offices in Toronto, Ontario. The referee gets on the phone to Toronto and waits while league officials review the call. This helps speed up the process and get back to the action fans came out to see.

CHAPTER 4

MOVE THE PUCK

It is hard to even imagine hockey without forward passing. One of the game's most exciting plays is a cross-ice pass to a streaking forward that creates a breakaway. But until 1929, that play was illegal. Forward passing was against the rules.

In the early 1920s, the league experimented with forward passes in a team's own zone or in the neutral zone. But in the offensive zone, all passes had to be backward. In order to score, a player then either had to shoot or take the puck to the goal himself.

That rule was changed for 1929–30. Forward passes became legal anywhere on the ice. The result was a massive increase in scoring. Until that season, no team had scored 100 goals in a season. Every team scored at least 100 goals in 1929–30. Few rule changes influenced the modern game of hockey like the forward pass.

caption: The forward pass is a fixture of hockey, but it was not always allowed in the game's history.

Montreal Canadiens right wing Bernie "Boom Boom" Geoffrion helped popularize the slap shot in the 1950s.

THE SLAP SHOT

A few hockey players claim to have invented the hardest shot in hockey: the slap shot. News reports from the 1930s and '40s discussed New York Rangers forward Alex Shibicky experimenting with the shot. But it may go back even further, to Nova Scotia in the early 1900s. Eddie Martin invented what he called a "baseball shot" playing for the Halifax Eurekas as part of an all-Black hockey league.

However, the player who popularized the slap shot in the NHL is Bernie Geoffrion. The power of his shot even gave him his nickname, "Boom Boom." Geoffrion was a high-scoring forward for the Montreal Canadiens dynasty of the 1950s and '60s.

The goal of the slap shot is to hit it so hard the goalie can't react in time. Shooters take a full windup with the stick, so the blade is high above their head. They then swing with all their might down through the puck.

With modern sticks, it is common now for slap shots to reach speeds of more than 100 mph (161 km/h). Boston Bruins defender Zdeno Chara set a record in 2012 for the hardest shot. His slapper traveled at 108.8 mph (175.1 km/h).

THE TRAP

A lot of the innovations in hockey have been designed to increase scoring. Not as many have been designed to prevent the other team from scoring. The neutral zone trap was designed to do just that.

Despite rules trying to limit the effectiveness of the trap, it can still be a useful strategy.

Jacques Lemaire did not invent the trap. When Lemaire was a player with the Canadiens in the 1970s, he recalled his

team using it from time to time. But as coach of the New Jersey Devils in the 1990s, Lemaire was the one to perfect it.

The goal of the trap is for the team without the puck to stay in the neutral zone as the puck is carried up the ice. They

Many of the rule changes implemented in 2005 were designed to help keep the action moving.

try and shut down all available passing opportunities. They want to force the puck carrier to the boards in order to limit his options. Ideally, the offense has to give up the puck and the trapping team can take it the other way.

Lemaire coached his Devils teams to a Stanley Cup victory. The Devils were still trapping in 2003 after Lemaire had left, and they won another Cup with it. The trap was a successful strategy, but goal scoring in 2003–04 dropped to its lowest level since the late 1960s.

The league implemented a number of rule changes in 2005–06 with the hope of boosting offensive production. Some of the changes were aimed at reducing the effectiveness of the trap. Previously, teams were not allowed to make passes that crossed two lines. The NHL eliminated this rule, allowing for long stretch passes.

Referees were also asked to keep an eye out for obstruction penalties such as interference, holding, and hooking. These rules were sometimes enforced inconsistently, which helped trapping teams slow down puck carriers. But with less contact allowed, offenses were free to move. Games averaged half a goal more than they did before the rule changes.

CHAPTER 5

BETWEEN
THE PIPES

Goaltenders have the most unique job on the ice. They have special equipment. They don't skate much. They almost never score.

Their simple job—keeping the puck out of the net—has evolved a lot over the years. The position has changed as hockey has changed. In the early days of the sport, pucks stayed mostly on the ice. Goalies made saves with their sticks and leg pads.

But even in the days without slap shots and curved blades, goalies still sometimes got hit in the face. In 1930 Montreal Maroons goalie Clint Benedict took a puck to the face. It shattered his nose and collarbone. Benedict returned to the ice, but he did so wearing a leather face mask. The mask made it

caption: Jacques Plante helped popularize goalie masks in the NHL.

difficult for him to see the puck, so Benedict stopped wearing it after a few games.

Despite the great risk of injury, it took another 29 years for a goalie to regularly wear a mask. On November 1, 1959, Montreal Canadiens goalie Jacques Plante took a puck to the face. He went to the locker room and got a mask that he sometimes wore in practice. Canadiens coach Toe Blake would not let him wear it in the game. But Plante refused to play without the mask. Blake eventually gave in.

At first, other players made fun of Plante. They said he was not tough and was afraid of the puck. But slowly, other goalies started to wear masks. Full acceptance took a while, though. The last goalie in the NHL to play without a mask retired in 1974. Goalie masks today also include helmets to fully protect the head.

SCORING GOALIES

Ten goalies have scored goals, usually by shooting the puck the length of the ice into an empty net. But only one has scored on the opposing goalie. Nick Vitucci of the minor-league Charlotte Checkers was clearing the puck in a 1996 game against the Louisville RiverFrogs. The puck went right to RiverFrogs goalie Alain Morrisette, who went to shoot the puck around his net, but he shot it in instead. Since Vitucci was the last Checkers player to touch the puck, he got credit for the goal.

LEG AND KNEE PADS

Goalies have worn some leg protection since the very beginning of the sport. These pads came from cricket. They were made of leather and stuffed with animal hair or furniture stuffing. But leather absorbed water from the ice. These pads became very heavy throughout a game. Nonetheless, pads remained basically the same for many years.

Today most goalies wear padding made of synthetic materials such as foam and plastic.

Waterproof pads arrived in the 1980s. They were lighter, which made goalies more mobile on their skates. This also made it easier to enlarge the pads to the giant box-shaped ones seen today.

Leg pads were officially limited to being 12 inches wide per a 1925 rule. But by the 1990s, that rule was widely ignored. Goalies wore huge pads that wrapped around the sides of their legs. Goalies also wore bulky chest protectors and covered them with oversized jerseys. In a reaction to record-low scoring, the NHL mandated some changes for the 2005–06 season. The size of all goalie pads was reduced.

MANNING THE NET

The NHL also made rules restricting how goalies can play. Starting in 2005–06, a trapezoid shape was painted on the ice behind each goal. Goalies could only handle the puck behind the goal line if they were in this area. That kept the puck in play longer and created more chances for the offense.

How modern goalies play the position has changed dramatically over the years. Until 1917, goalies weren't even allowed to drop to the ice. And even then, most goalies stayed standing. The "stand-up" style of goaltending was dominant

Goalies are allowed to go behind the net but are limited to a small area.

Most goalies still use elements of the butterfly style because of its effectiveness.

into the 1970s. But it had its weaknesses. It left a lot of openings for players to score with low shots.

Hall of Fame goalies such as Glenn Hall and Tony Esposito developed a new style of goaltending. To make low saves, the goalie would drop down to his knees and kick his pads out to both sides. This looked like a butterfly shape, and it was called the butterfly style.

The first goalie to really perfect the butterfly was Patrick Roy of the Canadiens. Roy was very active in goal. He moved quickly to shut down any opening. Roy won 551 career games using the butterfly.

Most modern goalies use a hybrid style. They still use elements of the butterfly, but also change it up to give shooters a different look. Modern goaltending focuses on positioning and reaction to cut down angles and reduce rebounds.

The goalie position has had numerous innovations that have made it what it is today. The same is true for the entire game of hockey. Whether for safety or excitement, these changes have made hockey the sport fans love today.

TIMELINE

1830s
The oldest known hockey stick is carved out of a sugar maple tree in Nova Scotia.

1875
The first indoor hockey game is held at Montreal's Victoria Skating Rink on March 3.

1929
The forward pass is legalized in the NHL.

1930
Clint Benedict becomes the first NHL goalie to wear a mask in a game.

1954
The first Zamboni ice resurfacer goes to work in an NHL game.

1967
In response to players bending their stick blades, the NHL begins regulating curved sticks.

1991
The NHL becomes one of the first North American sports leagues to use instant replay review.

2001
The Easton company releases the first stick made entirely of composite materials. It quickly becomes the choice of pro players.

2005
The NHL makes several rule changes to increase offense, such as limiting the size of goalie equipment and allowing the two-line pass.

2015
The NHL introduces three-on-three overtime for tied regular-season games.

HONORABLE MENTIONS

NEW HORIZONS

Since Gary Bettman took over as NHL commissioner in 1993, he has tried numerous ways to grow interest in the sport. That included expanding the league to cities where there previously was not much interest in a winter sport. The NHL expanded into Florida, Texas, Arizona, and Tennessee in the 1990s. Kids growing up in these cities suddenly had NHL stars to watch up close, and this boosted interest in hockey.

SHE CAN PLAY

Women's hockey dates back to the late 1800s. But for decades, hockey was considered a sport for men. Women's hockey wasn't organized on an international level until the 1980s. The first women's world championship took place in 1990. Women's hockey received its biggest boost in 1998 when it appeared in the Olympic Winter Games. The United States beat Canada that year to win the first Olympic gold medal in women's hockey.

THANKS, BUT NO THANKS

Not all hockey innovations work. In 1996 Fox Sports had the rights to broadcast NHL games. It came up with a technology to make the puck appear to glow on TV, making it easier to see for people not used to watching hockey. But longtime fans didn't need any help to see the puck. They found the technology annoying and distracting. Fox lost its NHL rights in 1998, and nobody has tried the glowing puck since.

GLOSSARY

blade
The part of the stick that handles the puck.

blue lines
The lines on the ice that establish the offensive or defensive zones.

breakaway
A one-on-one opportunity for a skater against a goalie.

commissioner
The chief executive of a sports league.

composite
A material that is made of two or more different substances.

goal line
The line a puck must cross to count as a goal.

hybrid
A combination of two different influences or styles.

neutral zone
The area between the two blue lines.

officials
People whose job it is to enforce the rules.

overtime
An extra period of play when the score is tied after regulation.

playoffs
A set of games played after the regular season that decides which team is the champion.

sudden death
An overtime format in which the first team to score wins.

MORE INFORMATION

BOOKS

Ferrell, Giles. *Great Hockey Debates*. Minneapolis, MN: Abdo Publishing, 2019.

Kortemeier, Todd. *Total Hockey*. Minneapolis, MN: Abdo Publishing, 2017.

Myers, Dan. *Hockey Trivia*. Minneapolis, MN: Abdo Publishing, 2016.

ONLINE RESOURCES

To learn more about innovations in hockey, please visit **abdobooklinks.com** or scan this QR code. These links are routinely monitored and updated to provide the most current information available.

ABOUT THE AUTHOR

Douglas Hustad is a freelance author primarily of science and history books for young people. He, his wife, and their two dogs live in the northern suburbs of San Diego, California.